LANGUAGE ARTS INDEPENDENT PRACTICE SUPER SIMPLE!

 EASY-TO-USE IDEAS FOR SKILL REINFORCEMENT

 Phonemic awareness

 Vocabulary

 Phonics

 High-frequency words

 Reading comprehension

 Writing

 Spelling

 AND LOTS MORE!

ENOUGH FOR

4 activities for every week

OF THE SCHOOL YEAR

Managing Editor: Kelly Robertson

Editorial Team: Stephanie Affinito, Becky S. Andrews, Randi Austin, Diane Badden, Janet Boyce, Kimberley Bruck, Karen A. Brudnak, Kitty Campbell, LeeAnn Collins, Pam Crane, Mary Davis, Stacie Stone Davis, Lynette Dickerson, Deborah Garmon, Kathy Ginn, Theresa Lewis Goode, Ada Goren, Tazmen Hansen, Marsha Heim, Lori Z. Henry, Jan Lavallee, Debra Liverman, Dorothy C. McKinney, Thad H. McLaurin, Sharon Murphy, Jennifer Nunn, Mark Rainey, Mary Robles, Hope Rodgers, Deborah J. Ryan, Rebecca Saunders, Kathleen Scavone, Betty Silkunas, Andrea Singleton, Leanne Stratton Swinson, Donna K. Teal, Joshua Thomas, Allison E. Ward, Carole Watkins, Zane Williard

www.themailbox.com

Table of Contents

To use the table of contents as a checklist, make a copy of pages 2 and 3. Staple or clip each copy on top of its original page. Each time you use an activity, check its box. Start each school year with fresh copies of the pages.

Skills Index on pages 111-112.

Twist a Letter

Letter formation

Materials:
capital letter cards
pipe cleaners

A child chooses a letter card. He carefully twists and bends one or more pipe cleaners to form the letter shown on the card. When he is satisfied with his work, he chooses a different card and repeats the activity.

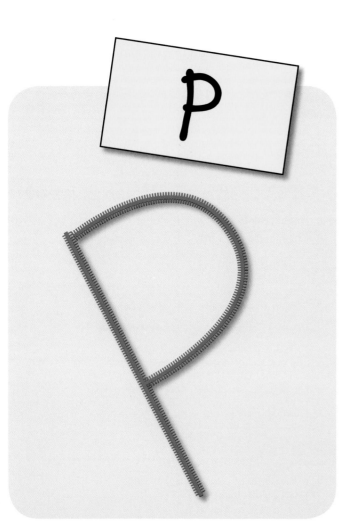

Roll and Write

Writing first and last names

Materials:
cube programmed with colored dots
blank paper
crayons

A youngster rolls the cube and finds the matching crayon. She uses that crayon to write her first and last name on a sheet of paper. She continues in this manner as time allows.

Name That Sound

Beginning sounds

Materials:
6–8 small objects
toy microphone

Possible objects include a book, cup, pencil, marker, hat, and fork.

A student chooses an object and says its name into the microphone. Then he says the object's beginning sound into the microphone three times before he repeats the name of the object. He continues in this manner with each remaining object as time allows.

Sing and Point

Letter recognition

Materials:
alphabet strip
alphabet cards, prepared as shown

A child points to each corresponding letter on the strip as he softly sings the alphabet song. Then he sings the song again, placing the corresponding alphabet card below the strip at the appropriate time in the song. For an added challenge, have him point to and name as many letters on the alphabet strip as he can without singing the alphabet song.

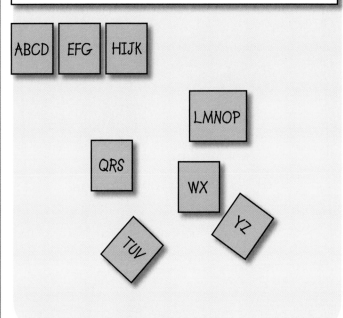

Fun With My Family

Oral language

Materials:
6" tagboard square
blank paper
crayons

A student traces the tagboard square on a sheet of paper. Inside the outline, she colors a picture that shows her family. Ask each child to tell you about her picture. Add her dictation to her work.

My daddy took me for ice cream.

Julia

On a Roll

Letter formation

Materials:
play dough
laminated letter cards

A child chooses a letter card. She rolls play dough into snake shapes and uses the shapes to form the uppercase and lowercase letters on her card. As the youngster uses her index finger to trace each play dough shape, she names the letter. Then she removes the play dough and repeats the activity with a different letter card.

Silly Snacks

Beginning sounds

Materials:
student copies of page 76
blank paper
scissors
glue

A student cuts out the cards. To choose a snack for each animal, she matches the beginning sound of the snack to the beginning sound of the animal's name. Then she glues the pairs of cards on a sheet of paper as shown.

By the Letter

Name spelling

Materials:
magazines
blank paper
scissors
glue

A youngster cuts from the magazine the individual letters he needs to spell his name. He glues the letters on the blank paper so his name is spelled correctly. Next, he cuts out magazine pictures that show things he likes and glues the cutouts around his name.

Packing Lunch

Sorting by category

Materials:
copy of page 77, cut apart
2 lunch-size paper bags labeled as shown

A child chooses a card. She determines if the sandwich is labeled with a number or a letter and then places it in the appropriate bag. She continues in this manner until each card has been sorted.

Ticket, Please!

Color words

Materials:
copy of page 78 prepared as shown

A youngster matches each ticket to the airplane in the corresponding color. For an added challenge, she chooses a ticket and copies the color word in the center of a blank sheet of paper. Then she draws items of the corresponding color around the word.

Snacktime

Beginning sounds

Materials:
paper plates (one per child)
half-sheets of blank paper
crayons
scissors
glue

A student decorates the plate to resemble himself with his mouth open. On blank paper, he draws a picture of a food item that begins with the same sound as his name. Then he cuts out the food item and glues it to the open mouth on his likeness.

Spell It Out

Name recognition

Materials:
class set of student name cards
metal cookie sheet
magnetic letters

A child chooses a card and uses magnetic letters to copy the name on the cookie sheet. When he is finished, he says the name he spelled. Then he removes the letters and chooses a new card to repeat the activity. He continues in this manner as time allows.

What's in a Name?

Letter recognition

Materials:
laminated poster listing student names
letter cards
wipe-off marker
paper towels

A youngster chooses a card and looks at the letter. Next, he looks at each name on the poster and circles each example he finds of the letter. Then he wipes off the poster and repeats the activity with a different card.

Nn

Say'Quan	Angelo
Holly	Owen
Ethan	Natalie
Tawana	Kim
Connor	Kendra
Bryce	Pedro
Mikayla	Nate
Tanner	Isabella
Sarah	Brandon

Everyday Objects

Matching words

Materials:
labeled classroom objects
cards programmed with words to
    match labeled objects

A student chooses a card and looks at the word. She finds the object that has the matching card and reads the word. She continues in this manner with each remaining card.

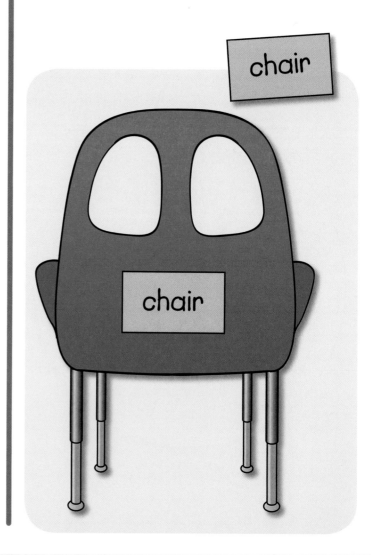

chair

chair

Word by Word

Segmenting sentences into words

Materials:
sentence strips labeled with simple sentences
pom-poms

A child chooses a sentence strip and reads the sentence. He places a pom-pom on each word. Then he counts the pom-poms to find out how many words are in the sentence. He continues in this manner with the remaining sentences.

Friendly Photos

Name recognition

Materials:
pocket chart with a class set of
    personalized photo cards
class set of student name cards

A student matches each name card to the corresponding card in the pocket chart. If time allows, she copies a name and draws an illustration of the chosen classmate.

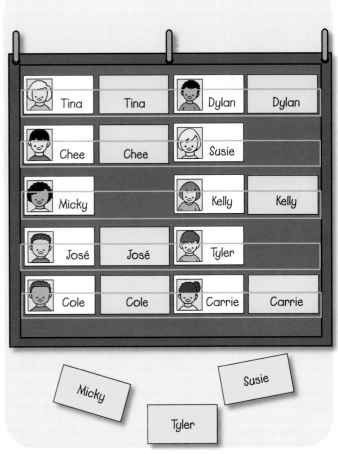

Picture-Perfect Puzzles

Literary response

Materials:
student copies of the puzzle pattern on page 79
familiar book
resealable plastic bags (one per child)
crayons
scissors

A student looks through the book and finds his favorite part of the story. He draws a picture of his favorite part on the puzzle pattern. Then he cuts apart the pieces, mixes them up, and assembles his puzzle. He stores his puzzle pieces in a plastic bag to take home.

Stamp and Trace

Letter formation

Materials:
word cards
blank paper
letter stampers
ink pad

A student chooses a card and uses the letter stampers to stamp the word on her paper. After her paper is dry, she carefully traces each letter using her best handwriting. She continues in this manner with different word cards as time allows.

Lots of Letters

Letter identification

Materials:
12" x 18" sheet of construction paper, labeled with a desired letter
container of colorful letter cutouts (several representing the featured letter)

A child chooses a letter from the container. If it matches the designated letter, he places it on the paper. If it does not, he sets it aside. He continues in this manner until he has sorted all the letters. For an added challenge, also label the paper with the lowercase version of the featured letter and place lowercase letter cutouts in the container as well.

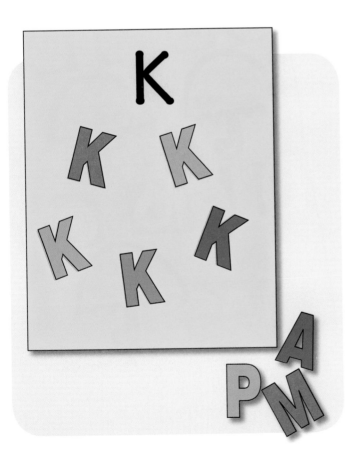

Writing Words

Handwriting

Materials:
photo album with magnetic pages
picture cards, placed in the photo album
sentence strip pieces (labeled in highlighter) to match each picture, placed in the photo album
wipe-off marker

A youngster looks at a picture and reads the word on the corresponding sentence strip piece. Then she uses the wipe-off marker to trace the word, using her best handwriting. She continues in this manner with the remaining pictures as time allows.

Search and Find

Letter recognition

Materials:
length of bulletin board paper, labeled
    with a letter and attached to a tabletop
magazines
scissors
glue

A child looks through magazines to find examples of the featured letter. When he finds one, he cuts it out and glues it onto the paper. He continues in this manner as time allows.

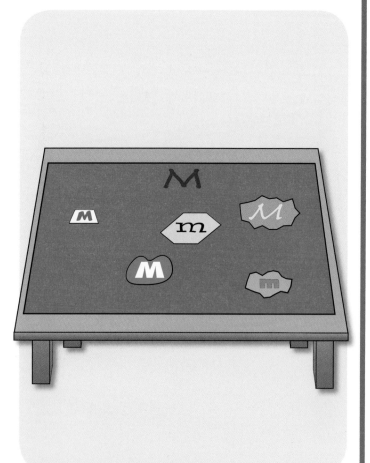

It's Raining Rhymes

Rhyming

Materials:
student copies of the picture cards on page 80
tagboard umbrella tracer (patterns on page 80)
9" x 12" light blue construction paper
    (one sheet per child)

A youngster divides a sheet of paper to make four sections. She traces the umbrella near the bottom of each section. Then she cuts out the cards and glues each rhyming pair in a separate section. For an added challenge, a child draws a picture on each umbrella to correspond with each rhyming pair.

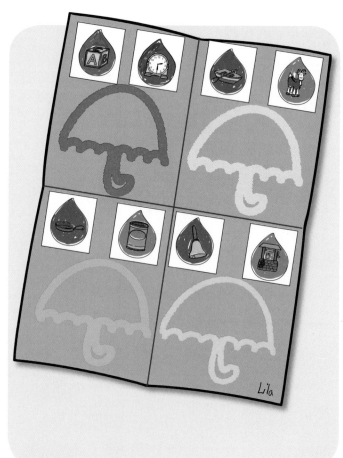

All in Order

Segmenting sentences into words

Materials:
pairs of identical sentences written on
 sentence strips, 1 strip cut apart
 into words and placed in a resealable
 plastic bag

A youngster places a sentence strip on his
work surface. He takes the words out of the
corresponding plastic bag and places each word
below the matching word on the sentence strip.
He continues in this manner with the remaining
sentence strips and bags.

B Is for Bag

Initial consonants

Materials:
lunch-size brown paper bag labeled
 with the letter *B* (one per child)
magazine pages
scissors

A student looks through the magazine pages
to find pictures of items that begin with the letter
B. When she finds an appropriate picture, she
cuts it out and places it in her bag. After she is
finished, she takes her bag home to share her
pictures with her family.

Sweet Treats

Color words

Materials:
colorful circle cutouts (lollipops)
jumbo craft sticks, each labeled with a
    featured color word in the corresponding
    color marker

A child matches each lollipop to the corresponding stick. Then he points to each stick as he reads each color word. For an added challenge, he draws on a sheet of paper a lollipop in his favorite color and labels it with the matching color word.

All Aboard!

Alphabetical order

Materials:
copy of the engine and caboose patterns
    on page 79, cut out
pocket chart
cards programmed with letters from *D* to *W*
alphabet chart

A student places the engine and caboose in the pocket chart, separating them as shown. Then she places the alphabet cards in order between them. She uses the alphabet chart to check her work.

Colorful Words

Spelling

Materials:
blank paper
highlighter
crayons

A student copies a word from the word wall onto his paper. Then he uses a highlighter to trace each letter as he spells the word. He uses a crayon to trace each letter as he spells the word a second time. He repeats this process with different words as time allows.

Wet Writing

Letter formation

Materials:
12" x 18" sheets of dark-colored construction
    paper (one per child)
letter cards
small cup of water
fine-tip paintbrushes

A youngster dips her paintbrush in the water and takes a card. Then she "paints" on her paper the letter shown on the card. She continues in this manner with the remaining cards. If time permits, she shuffles the cards and repeats the activity after her paper dries.

Fresh-Baked Cookies

Letter recognition

Materials:
26 brown tagboard circles (cookies),
   each labeled with a letter
cookie sheet
spatula

A child arranges six cookies letter-side down on the cookie sheet. Then he uses the spatula to flip a cookie. He says the name of the letter and then uses the spatula to remove the cookie from the cookie sheet. He continues in this manner with the remaining cookies. As time allows, he arranges new sets of cookies on the cookie sheet and repeats the activity.

What to Wear?

Days of the week

Materials:
student copies of page 81
24" lengths of yarn (one per child)
crayons
scissors
tape

A youngster decorates each T-shirt as desired. Then she cuts out the cards and tapes them onto a length of yarn in the correct order.

Sailing Away

Beginning sounds

Materials:
copy of page 82, cut apart
blue pond cutouts, programmed as shown

A child chooses a card. She says the name of the picture, emphasizing the beginning letter's sound. Then she "sails" the boat card on the appropriate pond. She continues in this manner until each card has been sorted.

How Many Letters?

High-frequency words

Materials:
student copies of a recording sheet, similar to the one shown
high-frequency word cards

A student chooses a card and reads the word. He determines the number of letters in the word. Then he copies the word in the appropriate column on his paper. He continues in this manner with the remaining word cards.

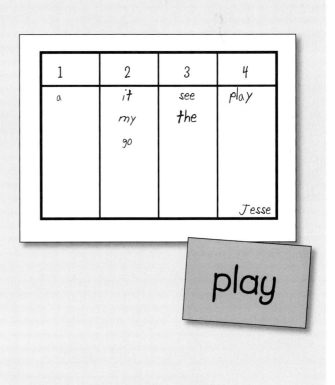

Orderly Shapes

Alphabetical order

Materials:
26 die-cut shapes, each labeled with a different letter
alphabet chart

A student randomly takes five shapes and identifies the letter on each. Then she puts the shapes in alphabetical order. She uses the alphabet chart to check her work. She repeats the activity as time allows.

Colorful Paints

Color words

Materials:
student copies of the watercolor paints
    pattern on page 83
crayons
scissors

A child reads each color word. Then he colors each circle the corresponding color. When he is satisfied with his work, he cuts out his paint set. For an added challenge, he chooses his favorite color and draws items of that color on the back of his paint set.

Memory Matchup

Rhyming

Materials:
construction paper copy of page 84, cut apart
pocket chart

A youngster shuffles the cards and places them facedown in columns in a pocket chart. He searches for a rhyming pair by randomly turning over two cards. If the two cards don't match, he turns them back over and flips two new cards. When he locates a rhyming pair, he removes the cards and places them side by side in his work area. He continues playing until all the rhyming pairs have been found.

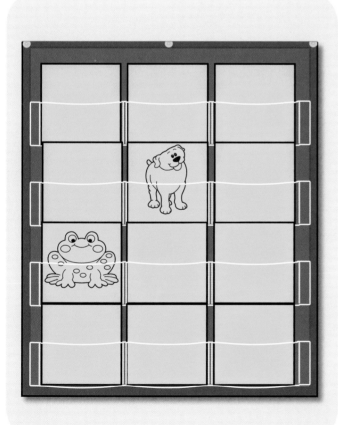

Character Booklet

Identifying the main character

Materials:
familiar book
blank paper
crayons

A child folds a sheet of paper in half and copies the title and author of the book on the front of the resulting booklet. She reviews the book and identifies the main character. Then she opens the booklet and draws a picture of the main character inside.

Hop to It!

Letter recognition

Materials:
plastic lid
cards labeled with letters

For a variation on the game of hopscotch, a student chooses ten cards and lays them in his work area to make a hopscotch board as shown. Then he tosses the plastic lid onto a card. Beginning with the first card, he quietly reads each letter aloud until he reaches the lid. If the lid lands outside the hopscotch board, he reads every letter on the board aloud. He continues in this manner as time allows.

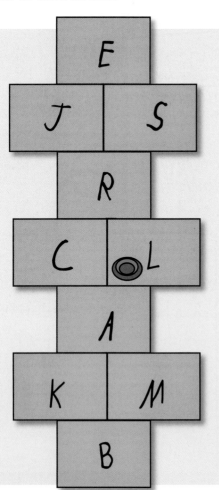

Clap and Sort

Syllables

Materials:
copy of page 85, colored and cut apart
2 paper plates, labeled as shown

A child names the picture on a chosen card and quietly claps out each part, or syllable, in the word. Then she places the card on the appropriate plate. She continues in this manner until each card has been sorted.

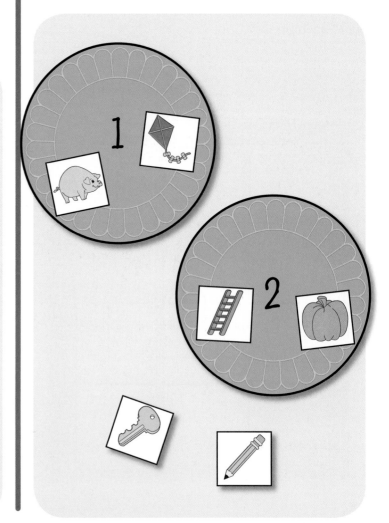

In the Mail

Spelling

Materials:
12 envelopes, each programmed with
   a picture card from page 84 and the
   corresponding word
appropriate letter tiles placed inside each envelope

A youngster takes an envelope, looks at the picture, and reads the word. He removes the letter tiles from inside the envelope and spells the word. Then he uses the front of the envelope to check his work and returns the letter tiles to the envelope. He continues in this manner with each remaining envelope.

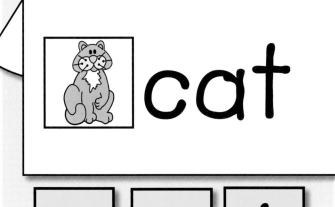

Look and Find!

Punctuation

Materials:
familiar books
plastic magnifying glass

A child chooses a book. She uses the magnifying glass to carefully look for ending punctuation on each page. She points to each example of ending punctuation as she finds it. She continues looking through the remaining books in this manner as time allows.

Cheese and Crackers

Uppercase and lowercase letters

Materials:
laminated cracker and cheese cutouts
   (patterns on page 83)
pairs of uppercase and lowercase letter cards
wipe-off marker

A student chooses an uppercase letter card and uses the wipe-off marker to copy it onto the cracker cutout. Then she finds the matching lowercase letter card and uses the wipe-off marker to write the letter on the cheese slice. She stacks her cracker and cheese slice to make a snack. She wipes off the cracker and cheese and repeats the activity with different letter pairs as time allows.

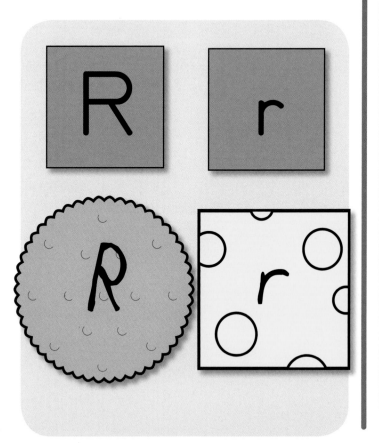

Sound It Out

Phonetic spelling

Materials:
blank paper
magazines

A student cuts a picture from a magazine and glues it to the center of a sheet of paper. From the picture, she draws four or five lines with circles at the ends. Inside each of these circles she writes a word to tell about the picture, using phonetic spelling to sound out each word.

Ready to Read

Parts of a book

Materials:
copy of page 86, cut apart
familiar books

A youngster chooses a book. Then he chooses a card, finds the featured element on or in his chosen book, and points to it. If the book does not have the featured element, he sets the card aside. He continues in this manner with each of the remaining cards.

Read, Make, and Write

High-frequency words

Materials:
student copies of a reproducible similar
    to the one shown
letter manipulatives

A child reads the first word on the list. She uses letter manipulatives to make the word in the corresponding section of her paper. Then she writes the word in the last column of her paper. She continues in this manner with the remaining words.

Ask or Tell?

Punctuation

Materials:
assorted period and question mark cutouts
2 sheets of construction paper, labeled as shown

A student sorts each punctuation mark cutout onto the appropriate paper. For an added challenge, she writes a sentence using an example of each punctuation mark on a sheet of paper.

In the Garden

Beginning sounds

Materials:
copy of page 85, cut apart
12" x 18" sheet of brown construction paper, prepared as shown (garden)

A child reviews the sound made by each letter in the garden. Then he says the name of the pictured item on each card, emphasizing the beginning letter's sound. He places each card in the appropriate garden row.

Piece It Together

Word families

Materials:
construction paper word family puzzle
    similar to the one shown
2 additional puzzle shapes, each labeled with
    a word not in the featured word family

A child spreads out the pieces of the puzzle and locates the word family piece. He reads the word on each remaining piece and places the corresponding pieces with the word family piece. Then he assembles the puzzle to check that his sorting is correct.

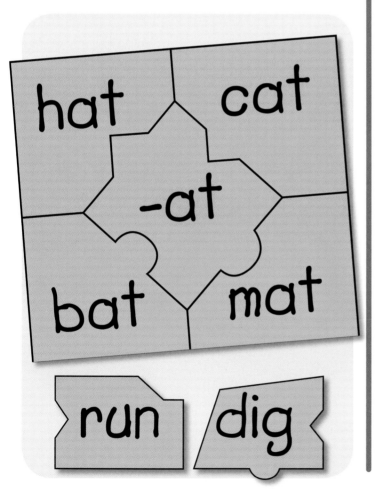

Tell All About It

Retelling a story

Materials:
stuffed animal
familiar books
blank paper
crayons

A youngster folds a sheet of paper in half to make a booklet. She copies the title and author of a chosen book on the cover of her booklet. Then she opens her booklet, draws her favorite character on the left side of the page, and draws her favorite part of the story on the right side of the page. When she is finished with her booklet, she uses it to help her retell the story to the stuffed animal.

Ring a Letter

Capitalization

Materials:
list of student names on tagboard
(some not capitalized)
rubber bands or elastic hair bands (one
for each name that is not capitalized)

A youngster reads the first name on the list. If
the name needs a capital letter, she places a band
around the first letter. If the name is properly
capitalized, she goes on to the next name. For an
added challenge, the child writes each name that
is not capitalized on a sheet of paper, correcting
the capitalization.

Names

bryson   kim
Jackson   Tyesha
Lila   Cindy
mindy   micah
Ben   Holly
doug   Kyle
Stefan   mollie
Randy   paco

Toss and Read

High-frequency words

Materials:
tagboard cutout labeled with high-frequency words
pom-pom

A child tosses the pom-pom onto the cutout
and quietly reads the word the pom-pom lands
on or is closest to. He continues in this manner
as time allows.

Write It Out

Alphabetical order

Materials:
26" lengths of adding machine tape (one per student)
letter manipulatives
alphabet strip

A student puts the letter manipulatives in order, referring to the alphabet strip as needed. When she is satisfied with the order, she copies each letter on the adding machine tape until she has written the alphabet.

Celebrate!

Creative writing

Materials:
construction paper
tagboard balloon tracer
yarn
scissors
crayons
tape

A student traces a balloon onto a sheet of construction paper and cuts it out. Then he draws a picture of a special celebration, such as a birthday party, on the front of his balloon. He cuts a length of yarn and tapes it to the back of the balloon cutout as shown. Then he writes about his picture on the back of his balloon.

What Happens Next?

Making predictions

Materials:
unfamiliar, wordless picture books
blank paper
crayons

A child opens a book to any page. She looks at the pictures and guesses what she thinks will happen next in the story. She draws a picture of her prediction on her paper. Then she looks at the rest of the book to see if her prediction was correct.

Make an Outfit

Uppercase and lowercase letters

Materials:
student copies of page 87, each shirt labeled with an uppercase letter and each pair of pants labeled with a corresponding lowercase letter
construction paper
crayons
scissors
glue

A child colors and cuts out the shirts and pants and scrambles them. He chooses a shirt, finds the matching pair of pants, and glues the resulting outfit on the construction paper. He continues in this manner with the remaining cutouts.

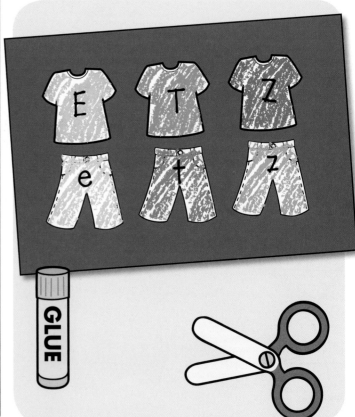

Crayon Pairs

Rhyming

Materials:
student copies of page 88
envelopes (one per student)
crayons
scissors

A student decorates an envelope so it resembles a crayon box and cuts out a set of picture cards. She matches the cards to make rhyming pairs and colors each pair a different color. Then she puts the cards in the crayon box to take home for additional practice.

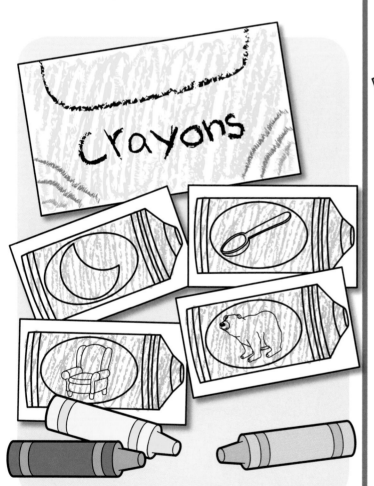

Read and Sort

Sorting words by category

Materials:
cards labeled with color words and shape words
two 12" x 18" sheets of construction paper
    labeled as shown
blank paper

A youngster sorts each card onto the appropriate sheet of construction paper. Then he makes a T chart on blank paper. He labels each column as shown and copies each word in the corresponding column.

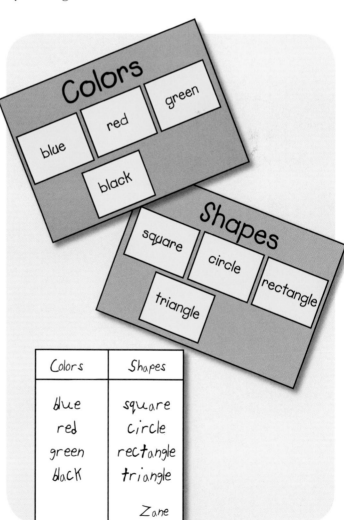

Set 15

I Spy

High-frequency words

Materials:
high-frequency word cards, displayed
 in an open area of the classroom
identical set of high-frequency word cards

A student chooses a word card and reads the word. He locates the matching word card in the classroom and reads the word again. He continues in this manner with each remaining card.

Roll and Color

Beginning sounds

Materials:
student copies of the gameboard on page 89
copy of the picture cards on page 89,
 cut out and glued to a cube

A child rolls the cube and says the name of the picture, emphasizing its beginning sound. Then she colors a picture on her gameboard that begins with the same sound. If there are no pictures remaining on her gameboard that begin with the corresponding sound, she rolls again. She continues in this manner until she has colored each picture on her gameboard.

A Fun Week

Days of the week

Materials:
student copies of the days of the week
cards on page 89
copy of the book *Cookie's Week* by Cindy Ward
8-page booklet (one per child)

A student reviews the book. Then he cuts out the days of the week cards, puts them in order, and glues one on each booklet page. He draws a picture of himself involved in a different adventure on each booklet page. On the booklet cover, he adds a title, similar to the one shown, and an illustration.

Family Tree

Word families

Materials:
blank paper
cards labeled with words, some from a chosen word
family and some from other word families
crayons

A youngster draws a tree on a sheet of paper. She writes the featured word family on the tree trunk. Then she chooses a card and determines if the word is from the featured word family. If it is, she copies the word onto the tree and draws a red circle around it so it resembles an apple. If it is not, she sets the card aside. She continues in this manner with each of the remaining cards.

What a Wardrobe!

Color words

Materials:
student copies of page 87, each shirt
labeled with a different color word
and each pair of pants labeled with
a matching color word
crayons
scissors
glue

A student colors a shirt and its matching pair
of pants the corresponding color. Then she cuts
out the pieces and glues them together to make
an outfit. She continues in this manner until she
has made six different outfits.

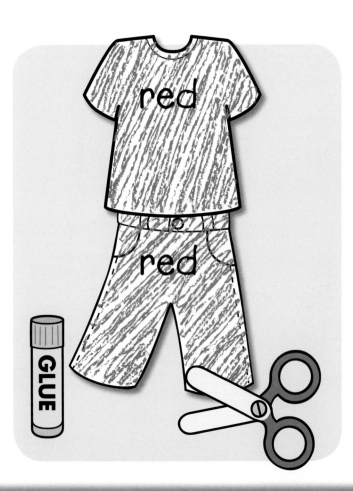

A Matched Set

Uppercase and lowercase letters

Materials:
fronts of greeting cards, each labeled
on the back with an uppercase letter
and its matching lowercase letter and
then cut in half

A youngster matches each uppercase letter to
the corresponding lowercase letter. Then he flips
the cards over to check his work.

Hats Off!

Rhyming

Materials:
tagboard hat tracer
blank paper
crayons

A child traces around the hat tracer on his paper. Then he draws on his hat two pictures that rhyme with *hat* and labels his illustrations.

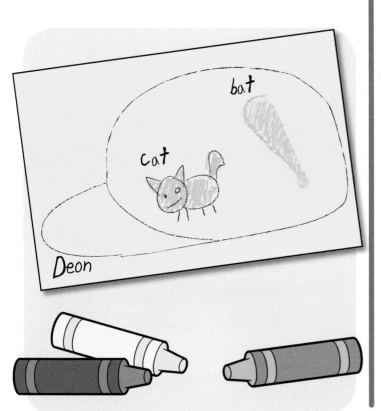

Grilled to Perfection

Punctuation

Materials:
copy of page 90, cut out
sheet of gray construction paper
    programmed with a grill grid
spatula
paper plate

A child places each steak on the grill. Then she reads each sentence and determines if the sentence has correct punctuation. If it does, she uses the spatula to move the steak to the plate. If it doesn't, she leaves it on the grill. For an added challenge, the child writes each sentence that remains on the grill, adding the correct punctuation.

Read and Tally

High-frequency words

Materials:
large heart-shaped cutout programmed with
    high-frequency words
familiar books

A student reads the words on the heart cutout. He looks through a book to find examples of the featured words. When he finds a word, he makes a tally mark beside the corresponding word on the heart. He continues in this manner as time allows. For an added challenge, a child writes a sentence using one or more words from the heart.

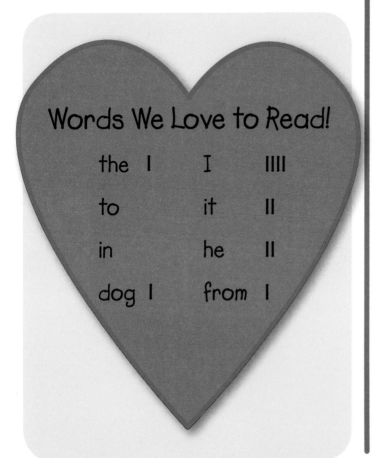

Words We Love to Read!

the	I	I	IIII
to		it	II
in		he	II
dog	I	from	I

Chip Dip

Word families

Materials:
yellow construction paper copy of page 91, cut out
two disposable plastic bowls labeled as shown

A youngster chooses a chip and reads the word. Then he places the chip in the appropriate bowl. He continues in this manner until each chip has been sorted.

tip   dip

-ip

hen

not
-ip

Flip Books

Initial consonants

Materials:
copies of page 92 (three cards per child)
blank paper
scissors
glue
crayons

A child folds her paper in half and makes two cuts in one of the halves to form three flaps as shown. She chooses three cards and glues each card to a flap. She says the name of each picture, emphasizing its beginning sound. Finally, she writes the beginning letter of each picture under each flap.

What's Inside?

Creative writing

Materials:
wrapped box containing a mystery object
sentence strip labeled with a sentence starter
blank paper
crayons

A child looks at the box and guesses what is inside. He draws a picture of his guess on his paper. Then he copies the sentence starter and completes the sentence.

I think a ____ is in the box.

Kyle

I think a teddy bear is in the box.

The Key Event

Literary response

Materials:
student copies of the key pattern on page 93, labeled
    with a book title before copying
a familiar book that matches the key
crayons
scissors

A student looks through the book to find an important event in the story. She draws a picture of the event on her key pattern. Then she cuts out the key.

Letter by Letter

Spelling

Materials:
cards labeled with spelling words
blank paper
letter manipulatives

A child chooses a card and uses the letter manipulatives to spell the word. Then he copies the word onto his paper. He continues in this manner as time allows. For an added challenge, the child turns his paper over and spells as many words from the front of his paper as he can without looking.

A Busy Day

Days of the week

Materials:
cards labeled with the days of the week
magazines
blank paper
scissors
glue
crayons

A youngster chooses a card and labels a sheet of paper with the name of that day of the week. Then she looks through magazines to find pictures of things she usually does on that day. When she finds a picture, she cuts it out and glues it to her paper. If she cannot find appropriate pictures, she draws her own illustrations.

In the Pond

High-frequency words

Materials:
student copies of page 94, programmed with one of the five words in the pond before copying
highlighter

A student reads the featured word. Then he reads each word in the pond. He highlights each example of the featured word he finds.

Familiar Words

Environmental print

Materials:
clean, empty food boxes and containers
cards labeled as shown

A youngster looks at the words on a food container. He determines whether he can read the brand name. Then he places the container beside the corresponding card. He continues in this manner with each of the containers.

Rhymes Inside

Rhyming

Materials:
small labeled objects
blank paper
crayons

Possible objects include a hat, pen, plastic mug, and block.

A child chooses an object. She folds a sheet of paper in half to make a booklet and draws and labels her chosen object on the front. Then she opens the booklet and draws two rhyming pictures inside.

To the Point

Punctuation

Materials:
student copies of a reproducible like the one shown
unsharpened pencil
ink pad

A child reads each sentence. Then he uses the pencil eraser to stamp a period at the end of each sentence that needs one.

Name _Ricardo_

1. I like to play.
2. My dog runs fast.
3. I see my mom.
4. The cat is soft.
5. The van is red.

Find and Circle

High-frequency words

Materials:
laminated copies of nursery rhymes in large type
high-frequency word list
dry-erase markers
paper towel

A youngster chooses a nursery rhyme and searches for examples of the listed high-frequency words. When she finds a featured word, she uses a dry-erase marker to circle it. She continues searching for words in this manner as time allows. When she is finished, she points to each circled word and reads it; then she wipes the marker off the nursery rhyme.

Word List

a	like
and	the
I	to
is	it
see	with

Hey Diddle Diddle

Hey diddle diddle,
The cat and the fiddle,
The cow jumped over the moon.
The little dog laughed to see such sport,
And the dish ran away with the spoon.

DRY-ERASE

Mystery Match

Uppercase and lowercase letters

Materials:
uppercase letter cards
container of lowercase letter manipulatives
writing paper

A youngster places five uppercase letter cards faceup in her work area. Then she pulls a lower-case letter from the box. If it matches one of her letter cards, she places it beside the corre-sponding card. If it does not, she sets it aside. She continues until she has matched each of the letters. Then she copies the resulting letter pairs onto a sheet of paper.

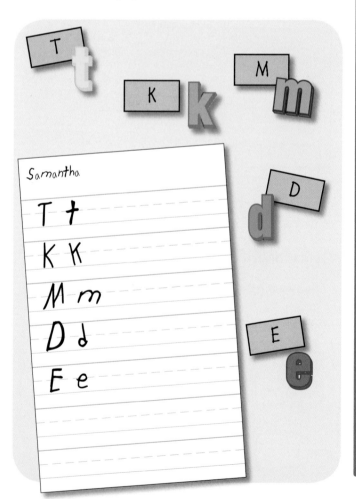

Category Collage

Sorting words by category

Materials:
9" x 12" sheets of construction paper (one per child)
cards programmed with categories
magazines
scissors
glue

Possible categories include foods, colors, shapes, clothing, and animals.

A student chooses a card and copies the cate-gory onto a sheet of paper. He cuts pictures of items from magazines that correspond with the category and glues the pictures to his paper.

How Many?

Syllables

Materials:
student copies of page 92
pom-poms
crayons
scissors

A child colors and cuts out her cards. She chooses a card and quietly says the pictured word aloud. She picks up a pom-pom for each syllable in the word. Then she flips the card over and writes the number of syllables on the back of the card. She continues with each of the remaining cards.

Cats Can!

Word families

Materials:
cat and can cards (patterns on page 93)
cards programmed with -at and -an words
blank paper

A youngster places the cat and the can on his work surface. He reads the word on each card and places it below the cutout with the matching word family. He continues until each card has been sorted. Then he makes a T chart on his paper and labels one column -at and the other column -an. He lists each word in the appropriate column.

Cover All

Uppercase and lowercase letters

Materials:
student copies of a 12-section grid
lowercase letter cards
game markers

A student labels each section of his grid with a different uppercase letter of his choosing. Then he chooses a card. If the corresponding uppercase letter is on his board, he covers it with a game marker. If it is not, he sets the card aside. He continues in this manner until each space on his board is covered with a game marker.

Caterpillar Parts

Sentence order

Materials:
resealable plastic bags, each containing a set of circles programmed with words to make a sentence
construction paper caterpillar head cutout
writing paper

A youngster places the caterpillar head on her work surface. She removes circles from a bag and arranges them behind the caterpillar's head to form a sentence. Then she reads the sentence and copies it onto her paper. She returns the circles to the bag and repeats the activity by choosing a different bag of circles.

G	P	K	S
L	M	O	D
A	F	Z	X

f

Beginning to End

Spelling CVC words

Materials:
student copies of page 95
scissors
stapler

A youngster cuts out the cards. She chooses a card and quietly names the picture, stressing the beginning and ending sounds. Then she writes the corresponding letters in each blank. She repeats this process with each of the remaining cards. Next, she stacks the cards in a neat pile. At an appropriate time, she asks to have her stack of cards stapled along the side.

Story Mobiles

Retelling a story

Materials:
construction paper strips (one per student)
familiar book
blank cards (three per student)
yarn
tape
crayons

A child copies the title of the book on the paper strip. Using the book as needed, he draws a story event on each card. Then he tapes a piece of yarn to each card and tapes each piece of yarn, in order, to the back of the paper strip.

Mail Call!

Initial consonants

Materials:
copy of page 96, cut apart
12 envelopes, each labeled with a letter

Label each envelope with one of the following
letters: *c, d, f, h, j, l, n, p, s, w, y, z.*

A student chooses an envelope, reads the
letter, and quietly says the letter's sound. He
finds the picture that begins with the corresponding sound and places it in the envelope.
He continues in this manner with the remaining
envelopes.

Family Pictures

Word families

Materials:
tagboard house tracer
blank paper
crayons

A child traces the house on a sheet of paper.
Then she writes a designated word family on the
roof of the house. Inside the outline, she draws
pictures of items from the featured word family.
For an added challenge, she labels each picture
with the corresponding word.

Space Stick

Writing a sentence

Materials:
jumbo craft sticks (one per student)
story paper
markers
crayons

A youngster decorates a craft stick so it resembles a person. Then she draws a picture on a sheet of story paper. She writes a sentence about her picture, placing the craft stick on the paper after she writes each word to ensure adequate spacing. She keeps her space stick available to use as she needs it.

Editor in Chief

Capitalization

Materials:
student copies of page 97
scissors
glue

A student reads each sentence on his paper. Then he cuts out the letters at the bottom of the page and glues the appropriate capital letter to the beginning of each sentence.

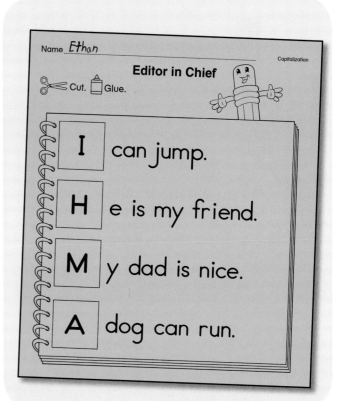

Take a Look!

Syllables

Materials:
decorated cardboard tube
bingo dauber
blank paper

A student looks through the cardboard tube as if it were a telescope. He looks around the classroom and finds an object to draw on his paper. He names the object and uses his hand to quietly tap out each part, or syllable, in the word. For each word part he hears, he uses a bingo dauber to stamp one dot next to his drawing. He repeats the activity with different objects as time allows.

A Memorable Game

High-frequency words

Materials:
pairs of high-frequency word cards

A child mixes up the cards and arranges them facedown in rows on her work surface. She flips two cards and reads the words aloud. If the words match, she keeps the cards. If the words are not a match, she turns the cards facedown in their original positions. She continues in this manner until she has matched each pair.

Keep It Cool

Nouns

Materials:
copy of page 98, cut apart
3 plastic cups, labeled as shown

A child looks at each card (ice cube) and determines if the picture shows a person, a place, or a thing. Then she sorts each ice cube into the appropriate cup.

Super Stamps

Writing a sentence

Materials:
variety of picture stampers
ink pad
writing paper

A youngster stamps a picture at the top of his paper. Then he writes a sentence about the object(s) he stamped.

How Familiar

Making text-to-self connections

Materials:
familiar books
sticky notes
blank paper

A student looks through a book and finds a page that reminds him of a situation in his life. He writes his name on a sticky note and sticks it to the page. Then, on a sheet of paper, he draws a picture showing his similar real-life situation.

Happy or Sad?

Capitalization

Materials:
sentence strips labeled with sentences, some without initial capital letters
smiley-face cutout
sad-face cutout

A child lays out the faces to begin two columns. She reads each sentence and determines if it is properly capitalized. If it is, she places it below the smiley face. If it is not, she places it below the sad face. She continues in this manner until she has sorted each sentence.

Cover and Circle

Initial consonants

Materials:
student copies of page 99
10 small pom-poms
scissors
stapler

A youngster cuts out the cards. Then he chooses a card, determines the beginning sound of the pictured item, and covers the corresponding letter with a pom-pom. He continues in this manner with the remaining cards. When he is satisfied with his work, he circles each covered letter and removes the pom-poms. Then he stacks the cards in a pile. At an appropriate time, he asks to have his stack of cards stapled along the side.

Change the Letter

Word families

Materials:
metal cookie sheet
the following magnetic letters: *b, d, f, h, j, m, o, p, r, t*
blank paper

A student places the letters *o* and *p* on the cookie sheet to form the rime *-op*. Then she places an onset (magnetic letter) in front of the rime. If it makes a real word, she copies it onto a sheet of paper. If it does not, she sets the onset aside. She uses each remaining onset to build a real or nonsense word in this manner. For an added challenge, a youngster repeats the activity with the rime *-ot*.

Right on Track

Story setting

Materials:
student copies of the train engine pattern on page 100
familiar book
blank 4" x 6" cards (one per child)
yarn
crayons
scissors
tape

A student copies the book title and author's name onto the train engine. Then he colors the train engine and cuts it out. He draws a picture of a setting from the book on a card. He tapes a yarn length to the back of the train engine and then tapes the opposite end of the yarn to his completed card so it resembles a train car.

In Full Bloom

Spelling

Materials:
tagboard flower petal template
cards, each labeled with the correct and an incorrect spelling of a word
construction paper
scissors
glue

A youngster traces the template onto construction paper to make a flower petal for each word card. He cuts out the flower petals and makes a flower center, a stem, and leaves. He looks at the word on each side of a card and turns the correct side faceup in a pile. He writes each correctly spelled word on one of the flower petals. Then he glues his pieces together to make a flower.

Race to the Finish

Word families

Materials:
copy of page 101, cut apart
length of masking tape labeled as shown and attached to the floor (finish line)

A child chooses a card and names the pictured item. If the word is part of the *-in* word family, he "drives" the card over the finish line. If it is not, he sets the card aside for a pit stop. He continues in this manner with each of the remaining cards.

Like *Cat* or *Pot?*

Short vowels *a* and *o*

Materials:
copy of the cat card on page 93, cut out
copy of the pot card on page 102, cut out
copy of the picture cards on page 102, cut apart

A youngster places the cat and pot cutouts on his work surface. He chooses a card and says the name of the picture, emphasizing the vowel sound. He places the card below the cutout with the matching vowel sound. He continues in this manner until each card has been sorted.

Set 26

Splish, Splash Stories

Creative writing

Materials:
light blue construction paper (one sheet per child)
writing paper
scissors
crayons

A student trims a sheet of construction paper to make a raindrop shape. Then she draws a picture of a rainy day on her raindrop. On a sheet of writing paper, she writes a sentence about her picture.

Give Me Five

Word families

Materials:
cards labeled with word families
letter cards
blank paper

A child traces his hand in the center of a sheet of paper. He chooses a word family card and writes the word family on the palm of his traced hand. He chooses a letter card and places it beside the word family card. If the combination makes a real word, he writes the word by one of the fingers or the thumb on his paper. If it does not, he sets the card aside. He continues in this manner until he has written five words (one beside each finger and the thumb) using the featured word family.

Find Four

Initial consonants

Materials:
magazine pages
letter cards
blank paper
scissors
glue

A youngster divides a sheet of paper into four sections. Then she chooses a letter card and writes the letter at the top of her paper. She looks through the magazine pages and cuts out four pictures that begin with the featured letter. She glues one picture in each section of her paper. For an added challenge, she uses inventive spelling to label each picture.

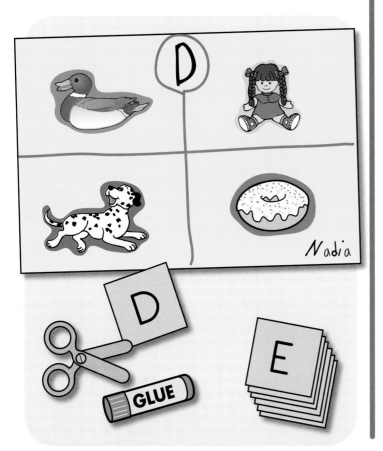

A Unique View

Writing a caption

Materials:
plastic sunglasses
story paper
crayons

A student puts on the sunglasses and looks around the room. When he sees something he would like to draw, he does so at the top of his paper. When he is satisfied with his drawing, he adds a caption to describe the scene.

Put It Together

Rhyming

Materials:
student copies of the puzzle piece patterns
   on page 100
construction paper (one sheet per child)

   A child colors and cuts out his puzzle pieces. He reads the word on each piece and matches the pieces to make rhyming pairs. When he is satisfied with his matches, he glues each pair onto a sheet of construction paper. For an added challenge, he draws a picture of his favorite rhyming pair on the back of his paper and writes a sentence about it.

Framed!

Main idea

Materials:
4½" x 5" squares of drawing paper
familiar book
craft sticks (four per child)
crayons
glue

   A student reviews the book to find the main idea of the story. She draws a picture of the main idea on a paper square. Then she turns her paper square over and writes a sentence about her picture. Finally, she glues craft sticks around her paper square to frame her picture.

Super Snapshots

Initial consonants

Materials:
paper squares programmed to resemble blank
  photographs
letter cards
tape

A student chooses a letter card and writes the letter on a paper square. Then he looks around the room for an object that begins with the letter. If he finds one, he pretends to take a photo of the item and then draws a picture of the object on his square to make a photograph. If he is unable to find one, he sets the letter aside. He continues in this manner to make several photographs.

Going Shopping

Writing a list

Materials:
grocery store flyers
strips of blank paper

A youngster looks through the grocery store flyers for items he would like to buy at the grocery store. When he finds an item, he copies the item's name on a strip of paper. He continues in this manner until he is satisfied with his list.

Set 28

What's the Letter?

Initial consonants

Materials:
6–8 small objects in a paper grocery bag
blank paper
crayons

Possible objects include a ball, book, cup, fork, hat, marker, pencil, and ruler.

A child divides a sheet of paper into four sections. She pulls an item from the bag and draws a picture of it in a section of her paper. She says the name of the item, emphasizing the beginning sound. Then she writes the corresponding letter above the picture of the item. She continues in this manner with the remaining three sections of her paper.

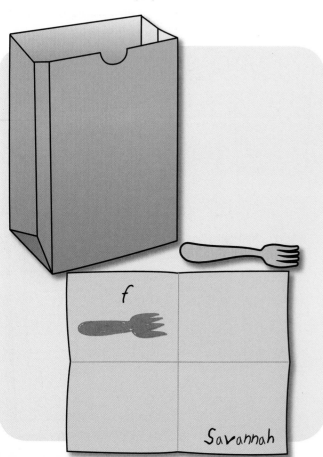

Real or Pretend?

Reality and fantasy

Materials:
stuffed bear or another stuffed toy
blank paper
crayons

A youngster writes the word *real* on one side of her paper. Then she draws a picture of the stuffed toy in a realistic situation. She turns her paper over and writes the word *pretend*. She draws a picture of the stuffed toy in a situation that is not real.

Under the Sea

Word families

Materials:
tagboard fish template
white paper circles (six per child)
light blue construction paper (one sheet per child)
letter tiles: *b, d, f, h, j, m, r, s*
glue

A student traces the fish template at the bottom of a sheet of light blue paper, adds desired details, and labels her fish with the word family *-ug.* Then she places one letter tile beside the word family. If the combination makes a real word, she writes the word on a white circle. If it does not make a word, she sets the letter tile aside. She continues in this manner with each remaining letter tile. Finally, she glues each of her labeled white circles above the fish to make air bubbles.

Doodle and Describe

Creative writing

Materials:
story paper
black marker
crayons

A child uses the marker to draw a doodle at the top of his paper. He incorporates the doodle into an illustration. Then he writes a sentence to describe his picture.

Read the Scoop!

High-frequency words

Materials:
student copies of the ice cream scoop pattern on page
    103, programmed with high-frequency words
matching high-frequency word cards
bingo dauber
triangle cutouts (one per student)

A student cuts out a scoop and glues it to a
triangle (cone). She takes a card and reads the
word. Then she uses the bingo dauber to dot the
same word on her ice cream cone. She continues
in this manner for each remaining card.

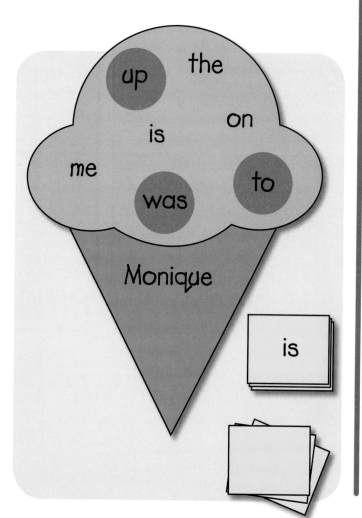

Cookie Cutter Scene

Creative writing

Materials:
cookie cutter
blank paper
crayons

A youngster traces the cookie cutter on his
paper. He colors the shape and incorporates it
into a scene. Then he labels or writes a sentence
about his drawing.

Book Buddies

Beginning, middle, and end

Materials:
student copies of page 104, programmed with the
    featured book's title
familiar book
construction paper
scissors
glue

A student reviews the book to determine the beginning, middle, and end of the story. Then he draws or writes to tell about each part in the corresponding spaces on his paper. To make a buddy, he cuts out the book pattern and uses the construction paper to add a head, arms, and legs.

Sound Sorts

Short vowels

Materials:
student copies of the picture cards on page 103
blank paper
scissors
glue

A student folds her paper in half and cuts out the cards. She glues the pig and duck cards on her paper to create column headers. Then she glues each remaining card in the column with the corresponding medial vowel sound. For an added challenge, she spells each word next to its picture.

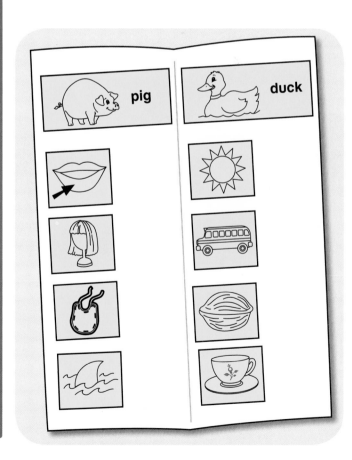

Fancy Flowers

Final consonants *m* and *t*

Materials:
student copies of the petal patterns on page 105
cupcake liners, labeled as shown (one of each per child)
2 different-colored crayons
scissors
glue

A student uses one crayon to color each petal that has a picture that ends with *m*. She uses the other crayon to color each petal that has a picture that ends with *t*. Then she cuts out the petals and glues them to make two different-colored flower heads.

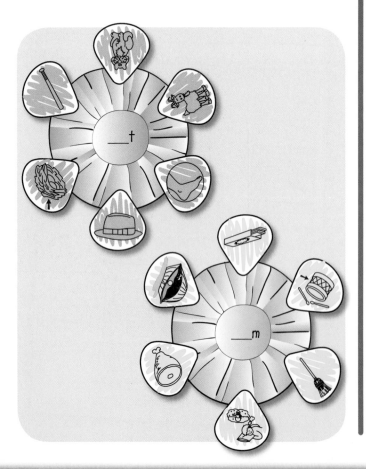

Me Too!

Making text-to-self connections

Materials:
familiar books
blank paper
crayons

A student selects a book and reviews the story. Next, he folds his paper in half and writes or draws about a story event that reminds him of a time in his life. Then he draws his personal connection on the other side of the paper.

George learns to ride a bike.   I learn to ride a bike!

Flip Flaps

Beginning, middle, and end

Materials:
familiar book
blank paper
scissors
crayons

A child folds a sheet of paper in half and makes two cuts in one of the halves to form three flaps as shown. She labels each flap as shown. Then she reviews the book to determine the beginning, middle, and end of the story. She draws or writes each part under the corresponding flap. Then she flips each flap to review each part of the story.

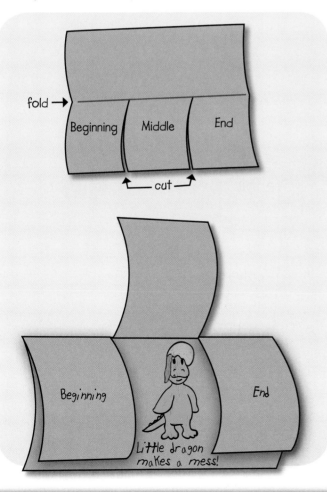

Over Easy

Short vowel e

Materials:
student copies of the yolk patterns on page 105
egg white cutouts (six per student)
spatula
yellow crayon
scissors
glue

A child colors each yolk that has a picture with the short *e* sound yellow. Next, he cuts out each yellow yolk and glues it to an egg white. He whispers the short *e* sound while he uses the spatula to flip each egg so that it is picture-side down. Then he uses the spatula to flip each egg picture-side up again and restates the name of each picture.

Fit for Royalty

Literary response

Materials:
student copies of the crown pattern on page 106
familiar books
paper strips (one per student)
crayons
scissors
glue

A student writes the title of a chosen book on his crown and illustrates his favorite part of the story. He cuts out the crown and glues it to the center of a paper strip. At an appropriate time, he asks to have his strip sized to fit his head.

Fill It In!

Initial consonants

Materials:
seven labeled objects or cutouts, initial consonants omitted
letter tiles that correspond with the missing initial consonants
writing paper
crayons

A student uses the letter tiles to complete the spelling of each object. Then he writes each word on his paper. He adds illustrations as time allows.

Sticky Endings

Punctuation

Materials:
paper strips programmed with simple sentences
 without punctuation
small sticky notes
blank paper
crayons

A student reads a sentence and determines if it is a statement or a question. She makes the corresponding punctuation mark on a sticky note and places it at the end of the sentence. She continues in this manner with each remaining strip. Then she writes and illustrates one sentence on a sheet of blank paper.

Magnetic Letters

Initial consonants

Materials:
cookie sheet
4 magnetic letters
blank paper
crayons

A child folds his paper to make four boxes. He lays his paper on the cookie sheet and places one letter on the left side of each box. Then he draws a picture of something that begins with each letter. To complete the activity, he traces each letter before removing his paper.

Wet Words

Spelling

Materials:
list of spelling words
paper towels
small chalkboard
paintbrush
cup of water
chalk

A youngster paints on the chalkboard with water to spell the first word on the list. Then he uses the chalk to spell the word three more times. He erases the board with a paper towel and continues in this manner for each word on the list.

A Strip of Reading

Word families

Materials:
long paper strips labeled with a desired word family (one per child)
letter cards
crayons

A student uses the letter tiles to create words in the corresponding word family. She writes each real word in green on her strip and illustrates it. She writes each nonsense word in red and draws a silly picture of the word.

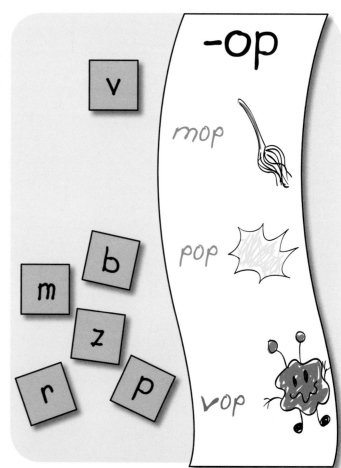

Who and Where?

Literary response

Materials:
multiple copies of the question cards on page 106,
    cut apart
familiar books
blank paper
crayons
glue

A youngster writes the title of a chosen book on his paper. He takes a card and glues it on the left side of his paper. Then he writes or draws to answer the question for the selected story.

Dreamy Stories

Creative writing

Materials:
dream-bubble cutouts (one per child)
blank paper
writing paper
crayons

A student draws a picture of a dream on her dream bubble. She glues it to her blank paper and draws a picture of herself sleeping. Then she writes about her dreamy drawing.

Set 33

Make 'em Move!

Action words

Materials:
copy of page 107, cut out
puppet or stuffed animal

A student takes a card and identifies the action. Then he uses the puppet to demonstrate the movement. He continues in this manner as time permits.

Letter Connections

High-frequency words

Materials:
Unifix cubes programmed with letters
list of high-frequency words
blank paper
crayons

A youngster connects the cubes to spell the first word on the list. Then she draws on her paper a corresponding-colored box for each letter cube. She writes each letter in its box and then reads the word. She continues in this manner with each remaining word.

Super Simple Independent Practice: Language Arts • ©The Mailbox® Books • TEC61147

Monster Face

Literary response

Materials:
copy of the monster key on page 108
familiar books
large circle cutouts (one per student)
supply of shape cutouts: circles, squares, and ovals

A student uses the monster key and selects the corresponding number of shapes for a chosen book. Next, she draws or writes on each of her shapes the appropriate story element. Then she glues each facial detail on a circle cutout to create a monster's head.

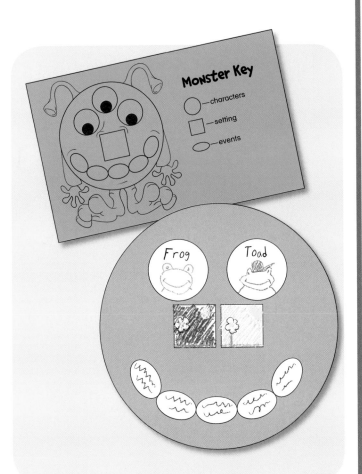

Beat the Clock

Ending sounds

Materials:
timer
6–8 objects
6–8 letter cards that match the ending sounds of the objects
blank paper

Possible objects include a cup, a crayon, a hat, a bag, a card, and a pencil.

A youngster starts the timer and quickly matches each letter card to the object with the corresponding ending sound. When finished, he records the time that it took to complete the task. Then he mixes the cards, rearranges the objects, and tries to beat his best time.

Is It Real?

Fiction and nonfiction

Materials:
copy of the fiction and nonfiction cards on page 108
fiction and nonfiction books
blank paper

A student uses the cards to sort each book into the corresponding category. Then he selects a book from each category and writes or draws on his paper to tell why he thinks it is a fiction or nonfiction book.

Sunny Sentences

Creative writing

Materials:
large yellow circles (one per student)
supply of yellow and orange triangles
crayons
glue

A youngster writes and draws on her circle (sun) to show what she does on a sunny day. Then she glues triangles around the sun so they resemble the sun's rays.

Spin and Spin

Blending words

Materials:
copy of the spinner patterns on page 109,
    prepared as shown
blank paper
crayons

A youngster makes a T chart on her paper. She labels one column with a happy face and the other with a sad face. Next, she spins each spinner. If the onset and rime make a real word, she writes the word below the happy face. If they do not, she writes the nonsense word below the sad face. She continues in this manner as time permits.

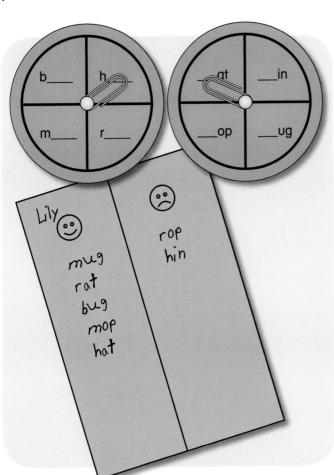

Toss for Sounds

Short vowels

Materials:
grid labeled as shown
4 pom-poms
blank paper
crayons

A youngster folds his paper to make four sections. Next, he tosses all four pom-poms on the grid and writes one letter in each section to show where the pom-poms landed. Then he draws a picture next to each letter that corresponds with its short-vowel sound.

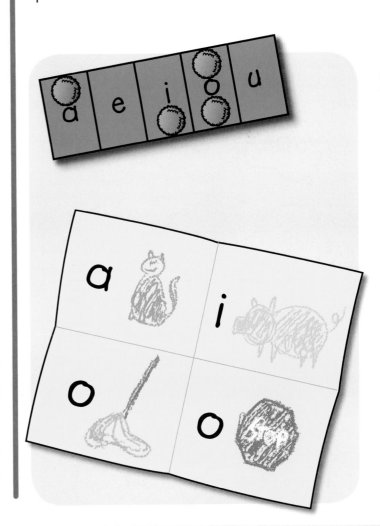

Set 35

Butter the Popcorn

High-frequency words

Materials:
white construction paper programmed with
    high-frequency words in popcorn
    outlines as shown
blank paper
yellow pom-pom
yellow crayon

A student reads each word and writes it on her paper. She draws a circle around each word. To "butter" the popcorn, she tosses the pom-pom onto the construction paper until it lands on a word. Then she reads the word and colors the same word yellow on her paper. She continues in this manner to "butter" each word on her paper as time permits.

Paired Up

Blending words

Materials:
piece of poster board, prepared as shown
2 pipe cleaner rings
blank paper
highlighter

A youngster drops a different pipe cleaner ring on each side of the poster board. Then he uses the letters in the onset and rime to make a word and writes it on a sheet of paper. If the word is real, he uses the highlighter to circle the word. He continues in this manner as time permits.

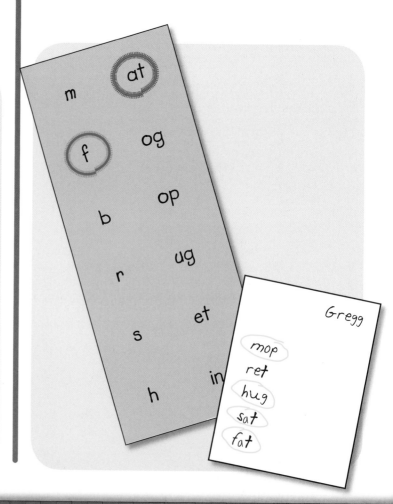

Chosen Objects

Creative writing

Materials:
2 bags, each filled with 6–8 labeled thematic objects
blank paper
crayons

Possible themes include shapes, animals, the beach, favorite books, toys, and school tools.

A student reveals the contents of a chosen bag and reads each word. Then he selects two objects and uses the words in a sentence. He writes and illustrates his sentence on his paper.

Sectional Scrapbook

Nouns

Materials:
magazines
3-column chart, labeled as shown (one per child)
scissors
glue

A youngster looks through magazines to find pictures that remind her of people, places, and things in her life. She cuts each picture out and glues it in the corresponding column on her paper. For an added challenge, she labels her pictures.

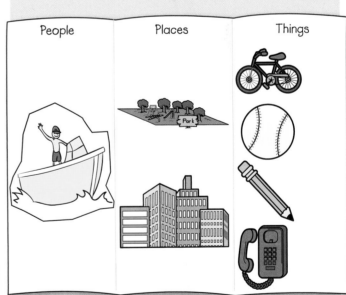

To the Jungle!

Action words

Materials:
student copies of the cards on page 110
copy of the spinner pattern on page 110,
    prepared as shown
3½" x 18" paper strips (one per child)
scissors
glue
crayons

A student cuts out her cards. She glues the lion on the left side of her strip and the jungle on the right side. Then she spins the spinner and draws the corresponding symbols to show how the lion moves toward the jungle. She continues spinning until her lion's path is complete.

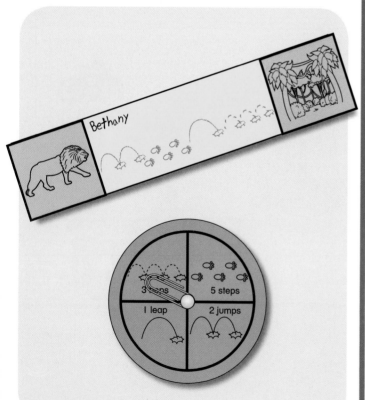

Inventive Endings

Extending a story

Materials:
familiar books
blank paper
crayons

A child folds his paper in half, unfolds it, and writes the title of a chosen book. After reviewing the text, he draws on one side of his paper to show how the story ended. Then he thinks about a different way to end the story and draws it on the other side.

Packed With Inspiration

Creative writing

Materials:
6–8 objects packed in a backpack
blank paper
crayons

Possible objects include a book, a flashlight, a ball, a camera, a drum, and a toy microphone.

A student pretends to go on an adventure and stops to rest. She empties the contents of the backpack and chooses one item that she will use on her journey. Then she writes and draws on her paper to tell how the item would be helpful to her during an adventure.

Alphabet Soup

Making words

Materials:
letter manipulatives in a pot
word cards
ladle
writing paper

A child scoops letters from the pot and takes a word card. He uses the letters to form the word displayed on the card. If letters are missing, he takes additional scoops. Then he writes the word on his paper. To continue, he returns the letters to the pot, takes a different card, and scoops letters to form and write each new word.

Picture Cards

Use with "Silly Snacks" on page 7.

TEC61147

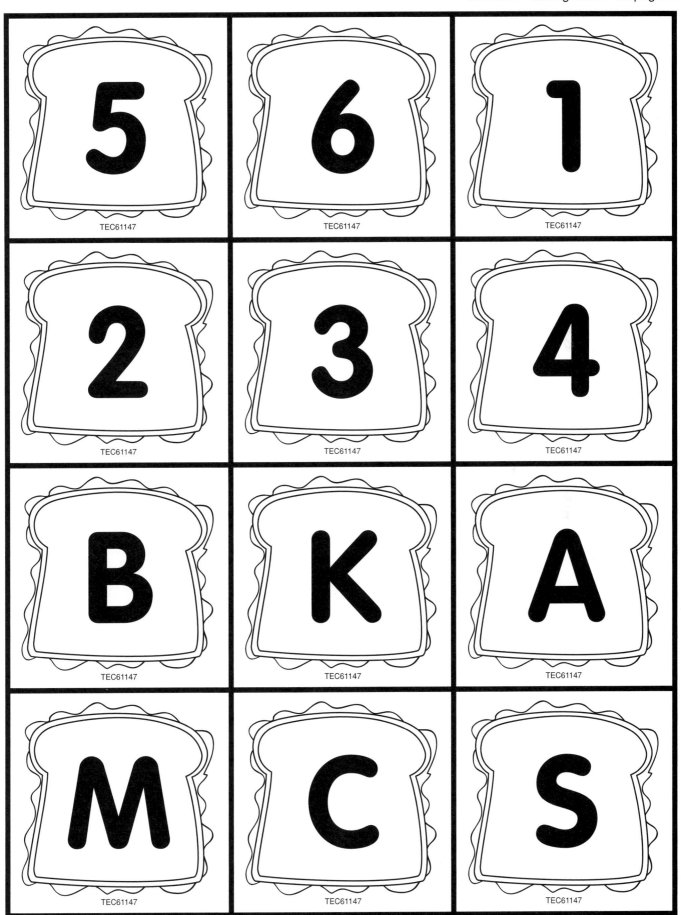

Airplane and Ticket Cards
Use with "Ticket, Please!" on page 8.

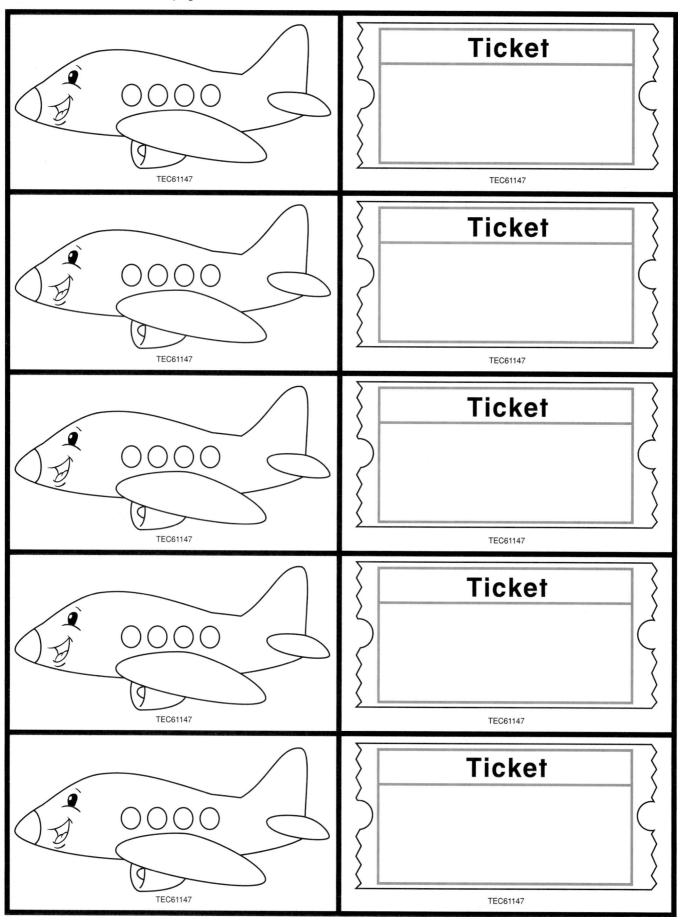

Super Simple Independent Practice: Language Arts • ©The Mailbox® Books • TEC61147

Puzzle Pattern

Use with "Picture-Perfect Puzzles" on page 12.

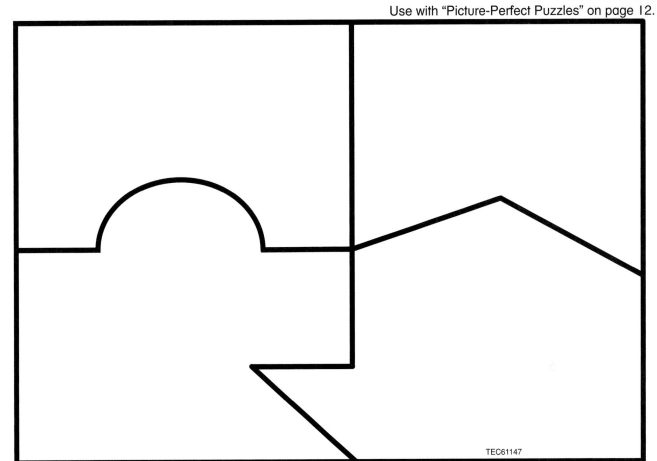

TEC61147

Train Engine and Caboose Patterns

Use with "All Aboard!" on page 16.

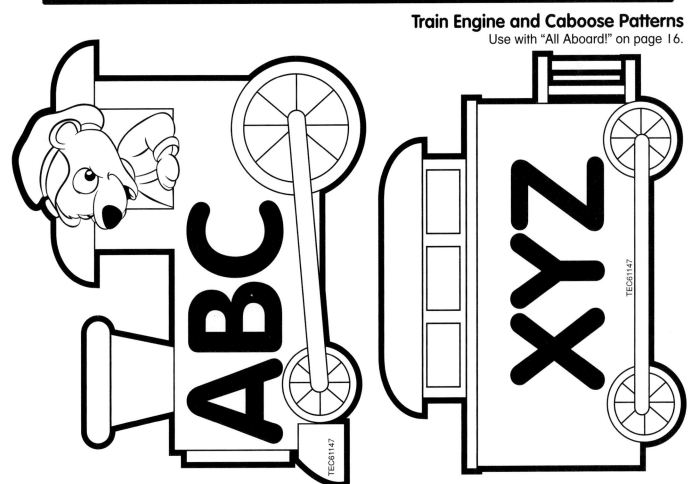

Picture Cards and Umbrella Patterns

Use with "It's Raining Rhymes" on page 14.

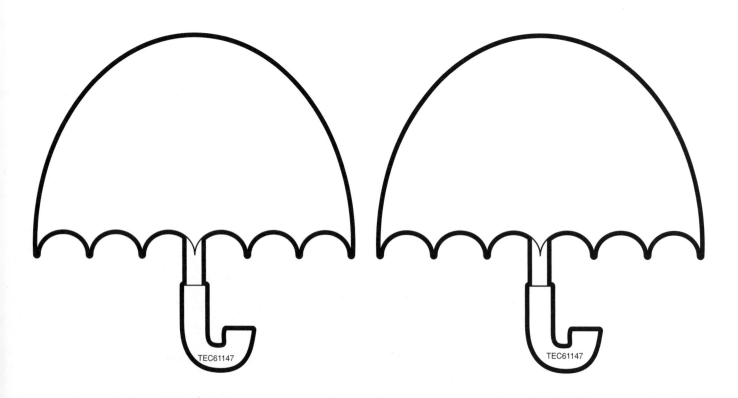

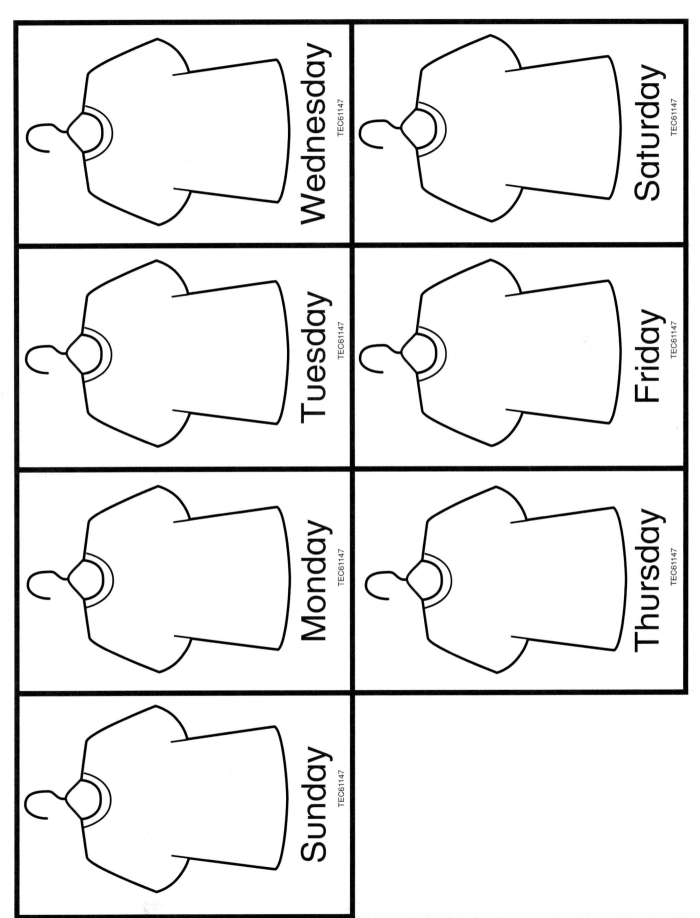

Wednesday
TEC61147

Saturday
TEC61147

Tuesday
TEC61147

Friday
TEC61147

Monday
TEC61147

Thursday
TEC61147

Sunday
TEC61147

Picture Cards

Use with "Sailing Away" on page 19.

TEC61147

TEC61147

TEC61147

TEC61147

TEC61147

TEC61147

TEC61147

TEC61147

TEC61147

TEC61147

TEC61147

TEC61147

Super Simple Independent Practice: Language Arts • ©The Mailbox® Books • TEC61147

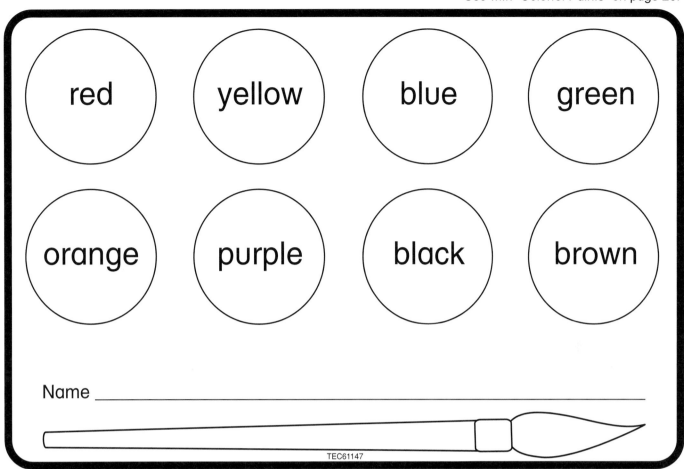

Name _____

Cracker and Cheese Patterns
Use with "Cheese and Crackers" on page 24.

Picture Cards

Use with "Memory Matchup" on page 21 and "In the Mail" on page 23.

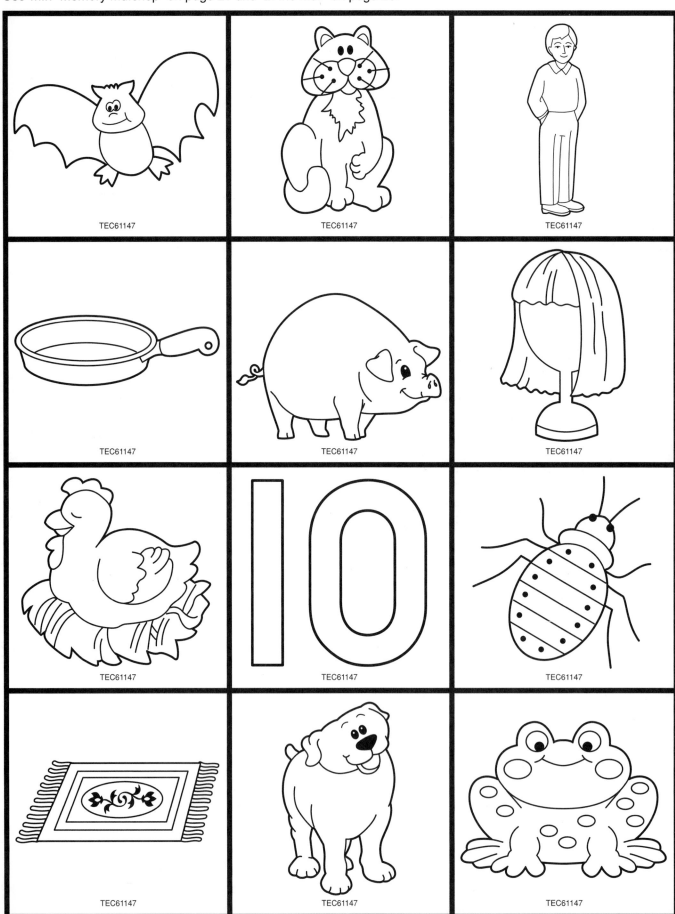

TEC61147

TEC61147

TEC61147

TEC61147

TEC61147

TEC61147

TEC61147

TEC61147

TEC61147

TEC61147

TEC61147

TEC61147

Super Simple Independent Practice: Language Arts • ©The Mailbox® Books • TEC61147

Use with "Clap and Sort" on page 22 and "In the Garden" on page 26.

TEC61147 TEC61147 TEC61147

TEC61147 TEC61147 TEC61147

TEC61147 TEC61147 TEC61147

TEC61147 TEC61147 TEC61147

front cover

back cover

title page

title

author

illustrator

Use with "Make an Outfit" on page 30 and "What a Wardrobe!" on page 34.

TEC61147
TEC61147
TEC61147
TEC61147
TEC61147
TEC61147

Picture Cards

Use with "Crayon Pairs" on page 31.

Super Simple Independent Practice: Language Arts • ©The Mailbox® Books • TEC61147

TEC61147

Gameboard
Use with "Roll and Color" on page 32.

Name _____

On a Roll!

Super Simple Independent Practice: Language Arts • ©The Mailbox® Books • TEC61147

Sunday
TEC61147
Monday
Tuesday
Wednesday
Thursday
Friday
Saturday

Steak Patterns

Use with "Grilled to Perfection" on page 35.

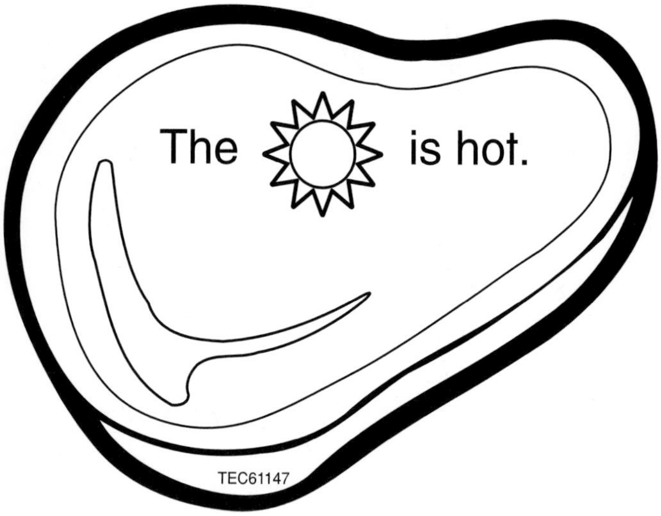
The
is hot.
TEC61147

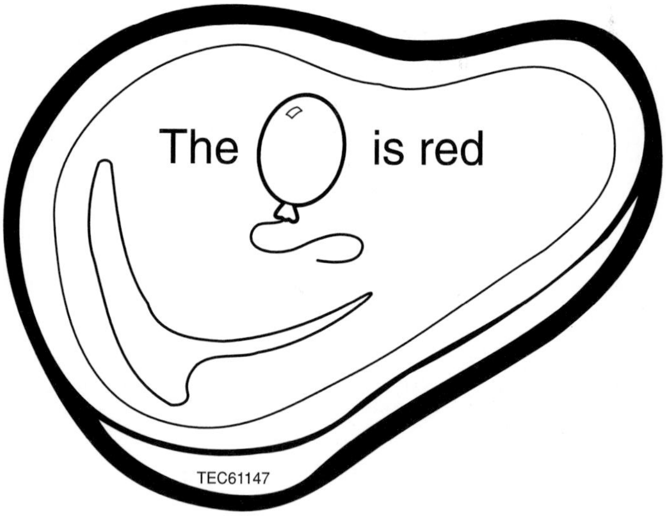
The
is red
TEC61147

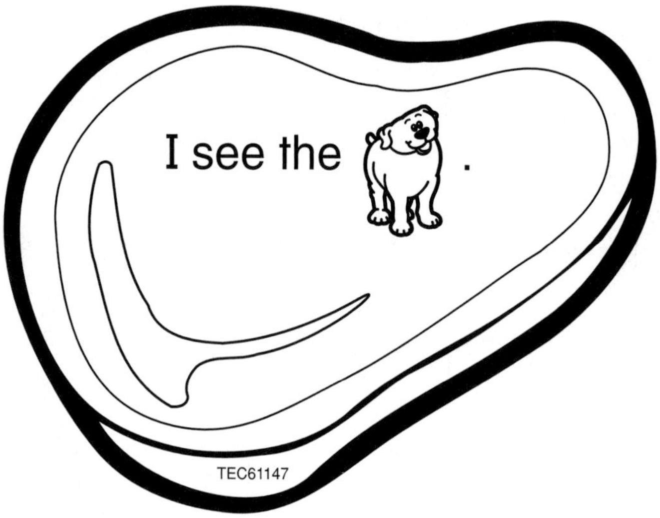
I see the
.
TEC61147

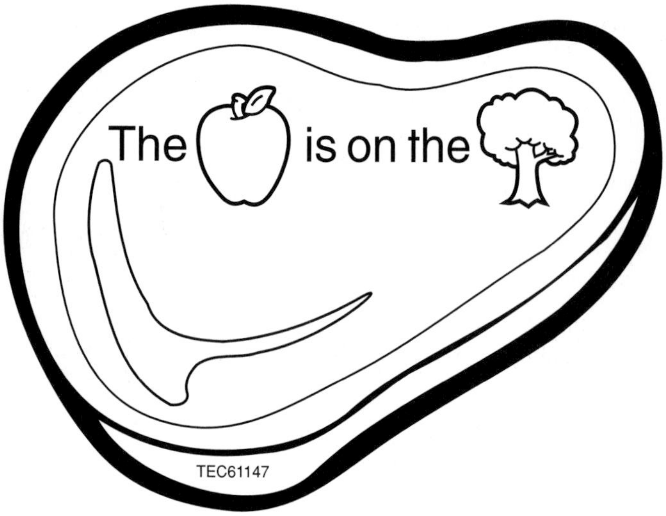
The
is on the
TEC61147

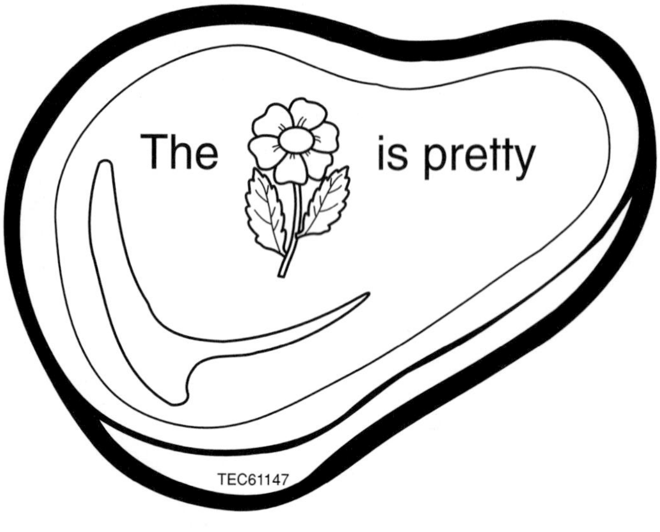
The
is pretty
TEC61147

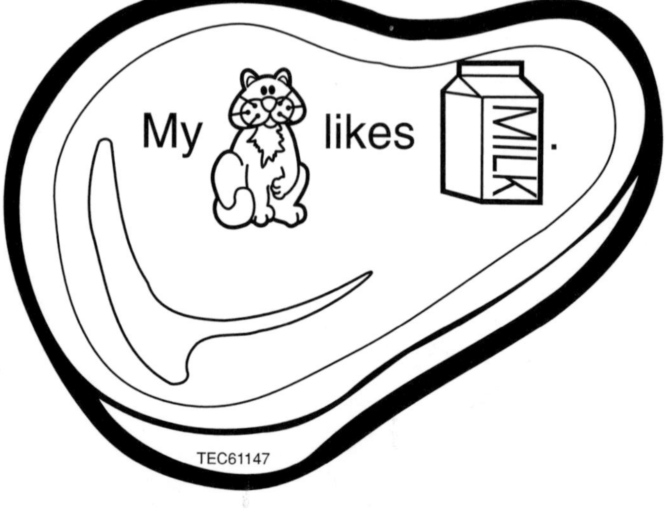
My
likes
MILK
.
TEC61147

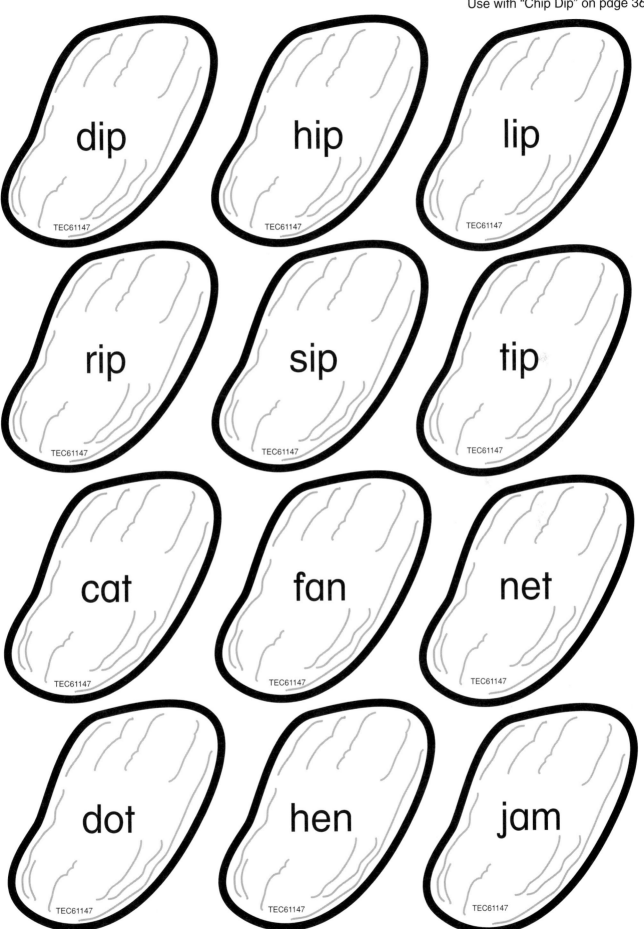

dip

hip

lip

TEC61147

TEC61147

TEC61147

rip

sip

tip

TEC61147

TEC61147

TEC61147

cat

fan

net

TEC61147

TEC61147

TEC61147

dot

hen

jam

TEC61147

TEC61147

TEC61147

Picture Cards

Use with "Flip Books" on page 37 and "How Many?" on page 43.

TEC61147

TEC61147

TEC61147

TEC61147

TEC61147

TEC61147

TEC61147

TEC61147

TEC61147

TEC61147

TEC61147

TEC61147

The Key Event

Book title:

_____

_____

TEC61147

Cat and Can Patterns
Use with "Cats Can!" on page 43 and "Like *Cat* or *Pot*?" on page 53.

cat

TEC61147

can

TEC61147

In the Pond

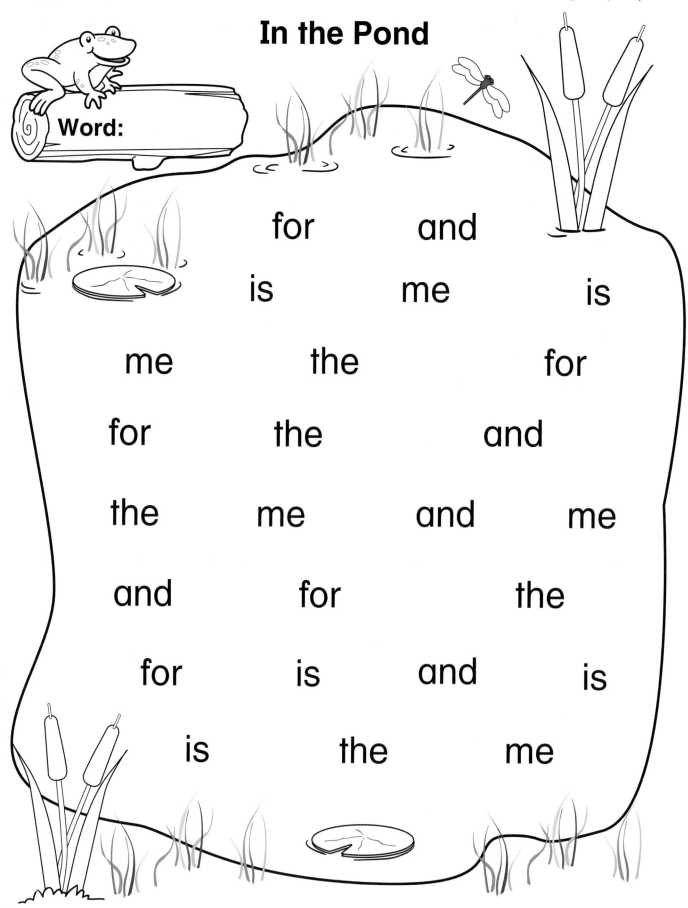

Word:

for   and

is   me   is

me   the   for

for   the   and

the   me   and   me

and   for   the

for   is   and   is

is   the   me

Super Simple Independent Practice: Language Arts • ©The Mailbox® Books • TEC61147

94   **Note to the teacher:** Use with "In the Pond" on page 39.

___ a ____   TEC61147

___ a ____   TEC61147

___ e ____   TEC61147

___ e ____   TEC61147

___ i ____   TEC61147

___ i ____   TEC61147

___ o ____   TEC61147

___ o ____   TEC61147

___ U ____   TEC61147

___ U ____   TEC61147

Picture Cards

Use with "Mail Call!" on page 46.

Super Simple Independent Practice: Language Arts • ©The Mailbox® Books • TEC61147

Editor in Chief

 Cut. Glue.

i	can jump.
h	e is my friend.
m	y dad is nice.
a	dog can run.

A I M H

Picture Cards

Use with "Keep It Cool" on page 49.

Super Simple Independent Practice: Language Arts • ©The Mailbox® Books • TEC61147

Train Engine Pattern
Use with "Right on Track" on page 52.

Name: _____

The Setting Train

Title _____

Author _____

TEC61147

Puzzle Pieces
Use with "Put It Together" on page 56.

wig   pig

TEC61147

boat   goat

car   star

dog   frog

Super Simple Independent Practice: Language Arts • ©The Mailbox® Books • TEC61147

TEC61147 TEC61147 TEC61147

TEC61147 TEC61147 TEC61147

TEC61147 TEC61147 TEC61147

TEC61147 TEC61147 TEC61147

Pot and Picture Cards

Use with "Like *Cat* or *Pot*?" on page 53.

pot

TEC61147

TEC61147   TEC61147   TEC61147   TEC61147   TEC61147

TEC61147   TEC61147   TEC61147   TEC61147   TEC61147

TEC61147   TEC61147   TEC61147   TEC61147   TEC61147

Super Simple Independent Practice: Language Arts • ©The Mailbox® Books • TEC61147

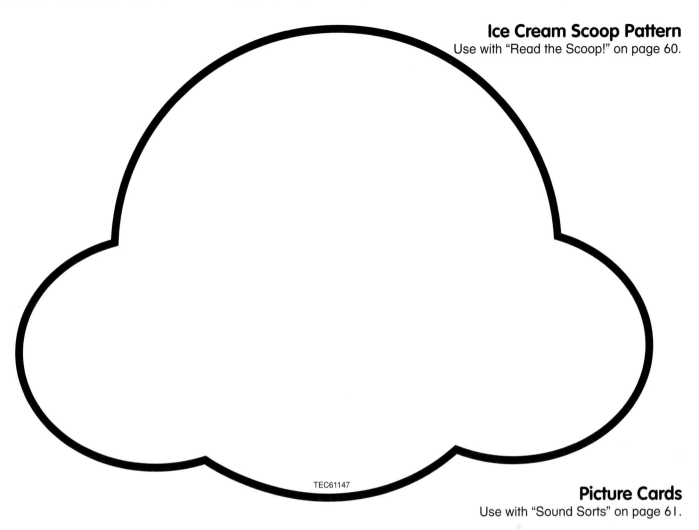

TEC61147

Picture Cards
Use with "Sound Sorts" on page 61.

TEC61147

pig

duck

Book Pattern
Use with "Book Buddies" on page 61.

_____
title of book

Beginning

Middle

End

TEC61147

Super Simple Independent Practice: Language Arts • ©The Mailbox® Books • TEC61147

Yolk Patterns
Use with "Over Easy" on page 63.

Crown Pattern

Use with "Fit for Royalty" on page 64.

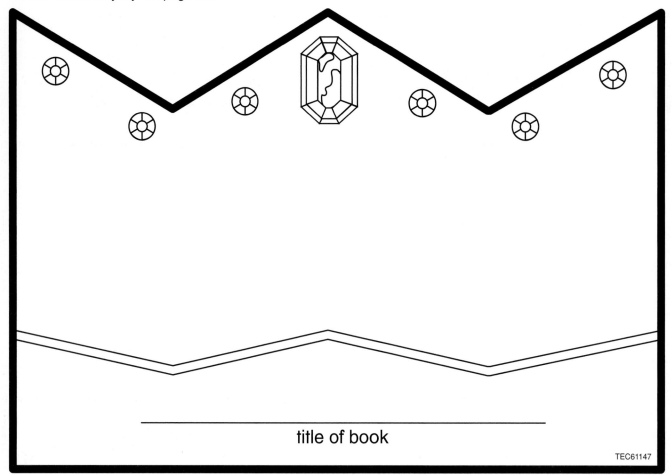

_____
title of book

TEC61147

Question Cards

Use with "Who and Where?" on page 67.

clap	crawl	cry
cut	dig	draw
drink	eat	hop
sleep	jump	kick
pull	ride	skip
sing	sit	snap
swim	talk	throw

Fiction and Nonfiction Cards
Use with "Is It Real?" on page 70.

Nonfiction

Real

TEC61147

Fiction

Not Real

TEC61147

Monster Key

◯ —characters

▢ —setting

⬭ —events

Super Simple Independent Practice: Language Arts • ©The Mailbox® Books • TEC61147

108   **Note to the teacher:** Use with "Monster Face" on page 69.

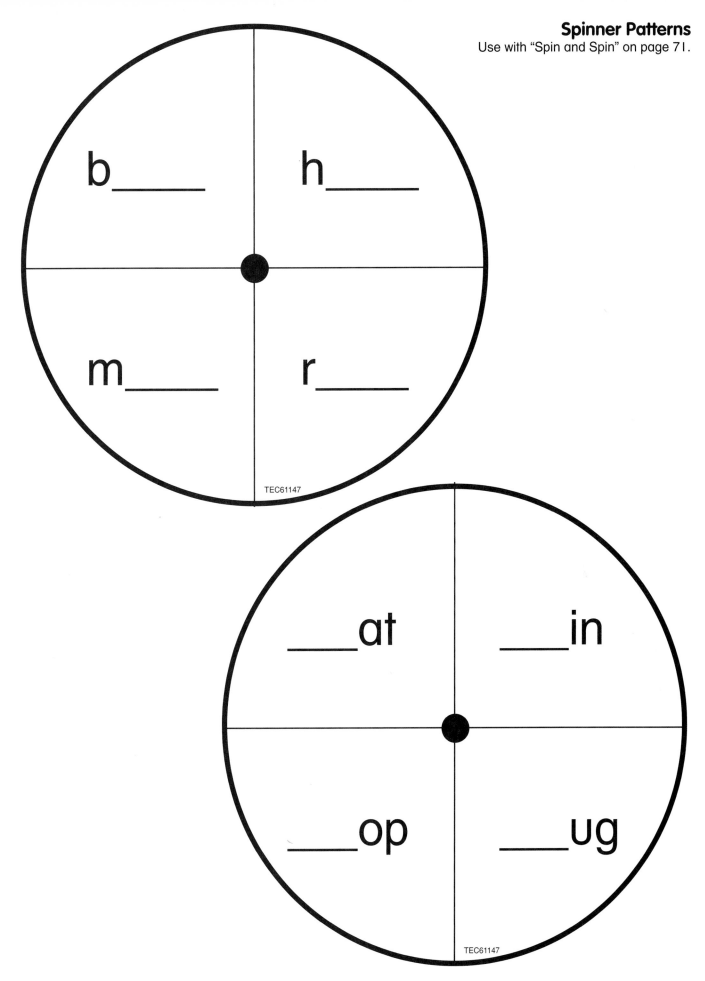

b_____ h_____

m_____ r_____

TEC61147

___at ___in

___op ___ug

TEC61147

Cards and Spinner Pattern
Use with "To the Jungle!" on page 74.

TEC61147

TEC61147

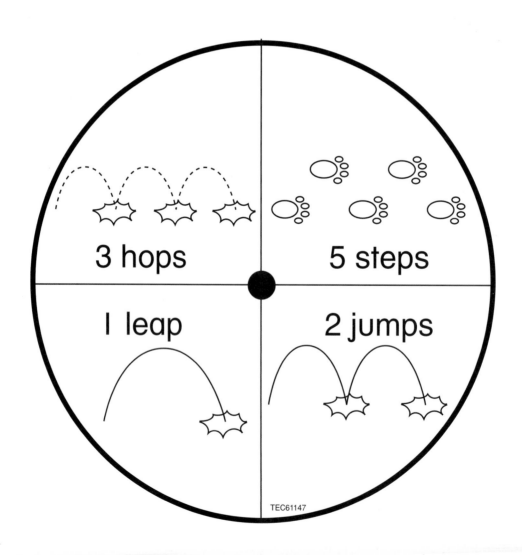

3 hops

5 steps

1 leap

2 jumps

TEC61147

Super Simple Independent Practice: Language Arts • ©The Mailbox® Books • TEC61147

Skills Index

Concepts of Print

Language Conventions

Phonemic Awareness and Phonics

Reading Comprehension and Literary Response